Movin

Essential Practical Advice

by Matthew Bazazi

Moving to the UK: Essential Practical Advice

First Edition

Disclaimer

This manuscript has been checked and is considered accurate at the time of publication. Send suggestions and feedback to movingbooksnews@gmail.com.

Website:

https://movingtolondon.blog

By the same author:

Moving to London: Essential Advice for Moving and Living on a Budget

For Tash.

Contents

1. Introduction

'It was many and many a year ago, in a kingdom by the sea, that a maiden there lived whom you may know, by the name of Annabel Lee.'

Edgar Allan Poe (1809-1849), author

Intended reader

The United Kingdom (UK) attracts people to it for all sorts of reasons. Regardless of reason, this book aims to help you by setting out the author's own experiences and synthesizing a wide range of resources to provide practical advice on all aspects of moving to and living in Britain.

It doesn't matter whether you are young or old, where you are from, whether you are just starting your working career, coming to study, changing careers or just want to experience the country. Moving can be simultaneously exhausting and exhilarating. My aim in writing this book is to make your move run a little smoother.

To help make the text readable I have focused on what makes the UK unique as much of what the UK offers is common to other countries. I have also added personal anecdotes and views where these are potentially helpful. This book does focus from time to time on London, reflecting the popularity of the city, however much of the advice can be applied across the country.

Throughout this book, I have sought to avoid providing long lists of resources for every topic covered, but instead, focus on general advice and helpful examples from the best of what's available. Other resources can be easily found online using a simple search. To avoid cluttering the text with web links, these are given in the Resources chapter at the back of the book. If you are reading the e-book version on a web-enabled device, you can click to open the website on your browser.

Finally, I believe that the UK's variety and the unstable economic picture can make providing estimates of likely costs misleading. For instance, rents have started to slide following a long period of year-on-year rises and it unclear how changes in the UK economy due to the European Union (EU) Referendum will play out. In addition, prices can quickly change and become out of date. Therefore, I have avoided providing numbers in all but a few places.

About me

I'm British born and bred, so I must provide the disclaimer that I did not move to the UK and I cannot share my own experience of moving here in this book. I grew up in Scotland and moved to London in 2013 so have direct experience of moving within the UK.

However, I do have the collective experience of the moves, many of my friends and family members have made to the UK over many years from around the world. This includes my wife and father, both of whom were born abroad and came to the UK to study. So, I have drawn upon their experiences in the writing of this book. My wife moved to the UK in 2005 to study medicine and currently holds Indefinite Leave to Remain (ILR) status, working towards applying for British Citizenship. My father moved to the UK in the early 1970s to study engineering and became a British Citizen in the 1980s.

In my personal and professional life, I have acquired knowledge of the UK's immigration system, so I have sought to simplify some of this information to make it accessible. All this information is freely available online and correct at the time of publishing. You won't find any insider secrets here.

If you are moving to the capital and are keen to save money, I have written a separate book '*Moving to London: Essential advice for moving and living on a budget.*' As the name suggests it is focused on moving to London and on money saving as the city can be very expensive.

Time to get going

I hope you will find this book both informative and enjoyable to read. Even if you find just a few of the sections here useful to you, I believe you will ultimately find this book to have been money well spent. You are probably only going to move to the UK once, so make the most of it and remember to enjoy each step along the way.

Good luck.

2. The UK in a nutshell

'Is it raining out? the reception girl asked brightly as I filled in the registration card between sneezes and pauses to wipe water from my face with the back of my arm. No, my ship sank and I had to swim the last seven miles.'

Bill Bryson (1951-), author

Reasons to move

The UK's high quality of living, social freedoms, education system and a melting pot of cultures make it one of the most attractive countries to live in the world.

You already probably know some of what there is on offer. Here are some other reasons you may not have considered to make this island your home.

- Generous holiday (compared to North America). British workers that work a 5-day week, have at least 28 days (5.6 weeks) of statutory leave, plus up to 8 public holidays each year. Many organisations offer more with the length of service.
- A short hop from Europe. It's quick and easy to travel to mainland Europe.

- Excellent national healthcare. The National Health Service (NHS) is a source of national pride and provides residents with a high-quality service that is usually free at the point of use.
- British sense of humour. In a nation that brought you *Monty Python*, *Fawlty Towers*, *Blackadder*, *The Office* and *Peep Show*, it's no wonder that Brits love sarcasm, irony and self-deprecating humour.

The UK's place in the world

Despite the country's small size, it continues to play a dominant role in world affairs. The UK has a long history and for better or worse has touched much of the world. While the country's physical presence is much reduced from its days of empire building, the nation's economy and cultural exports still provide it significant influence.

The UK's standing in the world may change following the EU Referendum result. Some say it will become stronger, unshackled by the bounds of Europe, while others would say its voice will diminish on the global stage. Time will tell.

EU Referendum

On the 23rd June 2016 the UK voted on a single question at the ballot box, *should the United Kingdom remain a member of the European Union or leave the European Union?* Most residents except European nationals were permitted to take part. The leave vote won by a small majority; 51.9% voted to leave, 48.1% voted to remain[1].

Britain's Exit from the EU, or simply Brexit is currently one of the most discussed topics in the UK and indeed around the world. The issue has divided British families and friends, although it has also brought into sharp focus just how many of us live in bubbles surrounded by others that hold similar views.

Voters intentions split along geographic, demographic, economic and social lines. To take just the geographic split, we saw within the UK, that England and Wales voted by a majority to leave, while Scotland and Northern Ireland voted to remain. Across the nation, towns and cities were more likely to vote to remain, while rural areas were more likely to have voted to leave.

[1] *EU Referendum results*. The Electoral Commission. https://www.electoralcommission.org.uk/find-information-by-subject/elections-and-referendums/past-elections-and-referendums/eu-referendum/electorate-and-count-information

At the time of writing the Brexit negotiations are underway and the details of what a post Brexit Britain will look like, have yet to be revealed. The UK will officially leave the EU on the 29th of March 2019. A transition period of up to two years, designed to allow the country to adjust, is expected to begin from this date. The details of the transition period are yet to be finalised.

The implications of Brexit on moving to the UK are numerous. This book sets out relevant facts as they are known at the present. It does not take a view on whether the result was the right or wrong decision. We all must live with the result, regardless of how we voted and make the most of what comes next.

There are those that might say the country is less welcoming to migrants than it used to be. In my experience, the UK is a tolerant place to live and people are generally interested in finding out about other nations, languages, cultures and particularly other cuisines. Yes, there are individuals that are less tolerant, that perhaps have been emboldened by the referendum result, however, they are a small minority and not unique.

The country in 2018 is not the same country of the 1950s or 1970s when many of its first generations of migrants settled. Among the nation's favourite foods are Indian and Chinese dishes, reflecting the prevalence of international flavours, a population plugged into global media and frequent holidays in the sun. These all reflect that the locals know more about the outside world than they once did.

What is clear is that many sectors of the UK economy are dependent on immigration. The majority of Britons welcome those who want to contribute, and the fabric of the country is a much more interesting place to live because of that.

Lay of the land

The UK, also known as Britain is actually a collection of nations; England, Scotland, Wales and Northern Ireland. Rather confusingly to visitors, the UK, a sovereign nation is referred to as a country, whilst England, Scotland, Wales and Northern Ireland are also considered countries. The individual countries are referred to as the home nations.

England is by far the largest and most dominant of the home nations on the world stage but all four countries have their own distinct qualities. England, Wales and

Scotland are collectively referred to as mainland Britain or Great Britain, while Northern Ireland is the northern part of the island of Ireland. Nearby islands including the Isle of Man, Jersey and Guernsey are considered Crown Dependencies while other former British Empire territories are referred to as British Overseas Territories.

Rivalries exist between the home nations but these are overwhelmingly friendly and similar to those found between neighbouring countries elsewhere around the world. Rivalries are often seen during the national sporting fixtures such as the Six Nations rugby tournament.

All the home nations, except England, have devolved administrations that devolve certain responsibilities such as tax and spending, education and justice to the nation. Wales has the Welsh Assembly, Scotland has the Scottish Government and Northern Ireland has the Northern Ireland Assembly.

There are stereotypes of the nationals of each nation and stereotypes of the British as a whole. Many of these are outdated or simply not true, while others contain a grain of truth. As with every nation, Britons may play up to certain stereotypes when discussing their country with others.

Stereotypes

It is said that behind every stereotype is at least some truth. The stereotypes you might have heard about the UK will depend on where in the world you are from.

- Here are some common aspects of British life.
- Nation of tea drinkers. Tea is popular, but a coffee culture has taken over and locals are now more likely to order a *Flat White* coffee than an *Earl Grey* tea.
- Buying rounds in the pub. Reciprocating a round is usually expected.
- Apologising at every opportunity. Brits love to apologise and will apologise if you bump into them or step on their top. Even if it was *your* fault.
- Standing in line. Waiting in line takes patience and Brits won't grumble for having to do so.
- Discussing the weather. If you are stuck for what to say, talking about the weather is a good bet.

Conventions

- Mains electricity is 230v at 50Hz. Plug sockets have three pins, adaptors are readily available from the airport or hardware stores.

- Measurements are a mixture of metric and imperial units. While metric measurements are becoming more common, the UK still uses imperial measurements such as stones and pounds for weight and miles for distance.

- Tap water is safe to drink. In some areas, particularly the south of England water has a high mineral content ('hard water') and this can be an acquired taste. Filters can be used to remove the minerals and neutralise the taste.

- Walking on the left. Most Brits will instinctively choose this side to walk down the pavement or staircase, reflecting the side of the road we travel down.

- The UK time zone is Greenwich Mean Time (GMT). Clocks go forwards one hour in the spring and back one hour in the autumn.

Economy

The UK's economy is highly developed and generates a high level of Gross Domestic Product (GDP). The service sector dominates the economy with financial services the most significant. Other sizable sectors include aerospace, pharmaceutical, tourism and energy industries.

Within the country, there are regional economic variations. The financial sector is concentrated in London, manufacturing is concentrated in the Midlands and the energy industries are concentrated in the north-east of Scotland.

The nation's economy is dominated by London and the south of England region. The economic dominance of the south of England is much discussed and many politicians would like to 'rebalance' the economy away from the south. In recent years the idea of a 'Northern Powerhouse' has been mooted to develop industries in the north of England and Wales, particularly through investment in transport links.

Weather

The UK has a temperate climate, similar to much of north-west Europe. The climate is strongly influenced by its proximity to the Atlantic Ocean and its latitude. Summers are usually warm and winters cool, with frequent light rain showers throughout the year. Average temperatures vary considerably between the home nations, with the warmest weather typically found in the south of England and the coldest typically endured in the north of Scotland.

Emergency services

In an emergency call 999 or 112. The operator will ask which service you require (police, ambulance, fire). For non-urgent medical assistance call 111.

3. Routes into the UK

'Mrs Brown says that in London everyone is different, and that means anyone can fit in. I think she must be right - because although I don't look like anyone else, I really do feel at home.'

Paddington Bear, Paddington film (2014)

Deciding your route

There is no right way to move to the UK. Your route depends on your circumstances, your nationality and what your future plans are. This chapter sets out the main ways that you can apply to come to the UK for a short or prolonged stay.

It is important to bear in mind that the country's immigration system is likely to evolve over the coming years in the light of the UK's decision to leave the EU. Initially, this will of course particularly affect current EU nationals but the whole system may evolve to meet the immigration demands of the country and political appetite for immigration. The government gateway website (https://www.gov.uk) is the usually best place to get the latest information.

It is recommended that this book is used as a starting point before undertaking more in-depth research. Once you have got an understanding and want to confirm and extend your understanding you could pay for advice from an immigration advisor. Seeking advice can be costly and by doing your research first this can hopefully allow you to seek focused professional advice. For instance, of the two routes you are considering which would they recommend. Or do they have any advice on how you can maximise your chances of success?

Visas are legal documents that allow entry based on a specific set of rules. Visas are issued by the Home Office, a UK Government department.

It goes without saying that you should follow the terms any visa you are issued. Failure to do so could mean removal from the country either immediately or in the near future.

The most common visas issued by the Home Office are for visits, followed by study visas and work visas. Strictly speaking, you may not wish to move to the UK if you are applying for a visitor visa however for the sake of completeness all visas will be described.

The UK will also accept individuals in desperate need, such as refugees however this route is not considered here.

Some general tips on applications

- If English is not your first language it is a good idea to make sure everything you have written makes sense. Don't assume anything and explain everything as clearly as possible. If possible, get a native English speaker to check the application.

- Ensure everything you include in the application is accurate to the best of your knowledge. Including deliberately misleading information could get you into difficulties.

- When completing your application form it is vital to provide all information required. If insufficient information is provided this could result in a delayed application.

- Maintain good records. You may be asked to provide evidence to verify your claims. Keeping paper records may help as they can be easily scanned or copied. Acquiring new documentation can be time consuming and it may not meet all the requirements you need. For instance, the electronic bank statements from your online banking may not go back far enough.

Every visa application has a service standard for the length of time a straightforward application will likely take. A straightforward application may mean no further information is required.

Service standard times can be found online and vary depending on whether applying for a visa, applying for settlement and if the individual is applying from inside or outside the UK.

By providing all the required information the first time, a visa application outcome should be given within the service standard time.

Visas can take months to hear back from. Certain visas can be fast-tracked by paying more, for instance for a one-day appointment.

European countries

The UK is leaving the EU on the 29th of March 2019. There will be no change to the rights and status of EU citizens living in the UK while the UK remains in the EU.

After the UK leaves there is likely to be a transition period of up to two years.

At the time of writing, the conditions for EU nationals arriving in the UK after the 29th March 2019 have yet to be confirmed.

Eligible EU nationals and their relations that arrive in the UK before the 29th March 2019 are encouraged to apply for Settled Status. Settled Status is a route to UK Citizenship.

Settled Status

- People who, by 29th March 2019, have been continuously and lawfully living here for 5 years will be able to apply to stay indefinitely by getting 'settled status'. That means they will be free to live here, have access to public funds and services and go on to apply for British citizenship.
- People who arrive by 29th March 2019 but won't have been living here lawfully for 5 years when we leave the EU, will be able to apply to stay until they have reached the 5-year threshold. They can then also apply for settled status.

- Family members who are living with, or join, EU citizens in the UK by 29th March 2019 will also be able to apply for settled status, usually after 5 years in the UK.
- Close family members (spouses, civil and unmarried partners, dependent children and grandchildren, and dependent parents and grandparents) will be able to join EU citizens after exit, where the relationship existed on 29th March 2019.

Acquiring Settled Status will prove that individuals have permission to continue living and working in the country.

The rules governing of EU nationals arriving in the UK after the 29th March 2019 have yet to be decided.

Countries in the European Economic Area (EEA) but not the EU, Norway, Lichtenstein and Iceland may or may not be eligible to apply for Settled Status.

The Schengen Area is a grouping of European states, mainly EU states that have officially abolished passport and border control at mutual countries. The UK is not part of the Schengen Area.

Commonwealth

The Commonwealth of Nations, (known simply as the Commonwealth) is an intergovernmental organisation of 53-member states around the world. Most of the members are former British territories such as Canada, Australia, New Zealand, Jamaica, Kenya, Nigeria, South Africa, India, Sri Lanka and Malaysia.

Citizens of the Commonwealth may have Right of Abode in the UK. The Right of Abode means that you don't need a visa to come to the UK and there are no time restrictions on how long you can stay for. All British Citizens have a right of abode in the UK.

Rest of the world

Most countries are of course not part of the EU or the Commonwealth. The UK maintains different relationships with different countries and can affect an application process.

Many countries do not require a visa to visit the UK. There are more than 50 countries and territories worldwide that do not require a visa to visit the UK for up to 6 months per year. For instance, for a holiday as a tourist. Working in the UK will usually require a visa regardless of where you are from.

Work visas

Work visas are issued to individuals that intend to work or volunteer in the UK. A range of work visas types are available, with the most common type is the Tier 2 (General) Visa.

The main categories of work visa are Tier 1, Tier 2 and Tier 5. The main purpose of each visa is given below, and each has a detailed set of requirements that can be found online. Detailed requirements can refer to aspects such as sponsorship, English language proficiency, income, savings, age, nationality, criminal and health records.

To apply for a Tier 2 and Tier 5 work visa you need to be employed by a licenced sponsor. A list of existing sponsors is available online and this is a good place to focus your efforts. Alternatively, you could apply directly to an organisation and ask them to become a sponsor organisation to allow them to sponsor you.

A smart way to come to the UK is if you already work for an international organisation that has a UK office using the Tier 2 (Intra-Company Transfer) visa. Your organisation would rather keep you than lose you, so you could apply to be transferred.

Tier 1

- Entrepreneur - setup or run a business
- Exceptional Talent - endorsed in your field in science, humanities, engineering, medicine, digital technology or the arts
- Graduate Entrepreneur - graduates that have a credible business idea
- Investor - want to invest a large amount of money

Tier 2

- General Visa - offered a skilled job
- Intra-Company Transfer - your overseas employer has offered you a UK role
- Minister of Religion - offered a job within the faith community
- Sportsperson - elite sportsperson or qualified coach

Tier 5

- Temporary Worker (Charity Worker) - unpaid voluntary work for a charity
- Temporary Worker (Creative and Sporting) - offered work in sport or in a creative role
- Temporary Worker (Government Authorised Exchange) - work experience or to do training, an Overseas Government Language Programme, research or a fellowship
- Temporary Worker (International Agreement) - work covered by international law while in the UK, for example working for a foreign government
- Temporary Worker (Religious Worker) - religious work
- Temporary Worker (Youth Mobility Scheme) - for those aged 18-30 years old

UK Ancestry Visa

Commonwealth Citizens with a UK-born grandparent can apply.

Study visas

Coming to study in the UK is a straightforward way to experience the UK first hand.

There are three types available.

- Short-term study visa - to undertake a short course of study
- Tier 4 Child Student Visa - to study at an independent school
- Tier 4 General Student visa - to study in the UK

Study visas are issued for the length of the course you are embarking on. The majority of those on study visas will return home after their course has finished. Some will decide to extend their stay by applying for a new visa, for instance, a visa for work or postgraduate study.

When applying for a postgraduate course make sure you are doing it for the right reasons. I have met international students who have applied for PhDs seemingly more because they were keen to stay in the UK, rather than because they wanted to take further study or research. It's important to take responsibility of your long-term career aspirations.

Eligibility for these visas include the offer of a place on a course at an appropriate level, an appropriate institution, have sufficient English language knowledge and the ability to fund your studies.

Family visas

A family visa can be applied to if you want to live with a family member in the UK for more than 6 months. For a stay of fewer than 6 months, a Standard Visitor visa is probably more appropriate.

A family member could be a spouse, partner, fiancé/fiancée/proposed civil partner, child, parent or relative you will provide long term care for.

Tourist and short stay visas

The main types of visa to visit the UK as a tourist or for a short stay are.

- Standard Visitor visa - visit for leisure, business or receive private medical treatment
- Permitted Paid Engagement visa - invited as an expert

- Marriage Visitor visa - want to get married or enter a Civil Partnership in the UK
- Parent of a Tier 4 child visa - parent of a child at an independent school
- Visit the UK in a Chinese Tour Group

The Standard Visitor visa is the most common way to visit the UK and can be issued for up to 6 months. The time permitted depends on the country.

Transit visas

A transit visa is used to pass through the UK on your way to another country.

Health Surcharge

All visa applications that are not for permanent settlement (Leave to Remain), must now pay a set amount towards the National Health Service. The amount is charged per year and must be paid upfront.

Once you have paid the surcharge, you are treated the same as other British residents, in that the NHS is generally free at the point of use. Across England, Wales and Northern Ireland most residents pay a nominal fee for NHS prescriptions and dental treatment. In Scotland, there is no charge for NHS prescriptions.

Biometric Residence Permit

If you are granted a visa for more than 6 months you will also receive a Biometric Residence Permit (BPR). A BPR is also sent if you extend your visa for more than 6 months, apply to settle, transfer your visa to a new passport or apply for certain travel documents.

The BPR card states important identity information about you including your biometrics. The biometrics include your fingerprints and photo.

The card is used to prove your identity and your rights in the country. Your rights include your right to study or work in the UK and access to benefits or public services.

A word of warning. As with all immigration documentation, keep it safe as and it can be both costly and time consuming to replace. My wife discovered this after having her bag stolen and it significantly added to the stress of the robbery. Only carry the card if you genuinely need it, not as a form of general ID, for instance, if you want to buy alcohol. If you need a general ID then apply for a provisional driving licence.

4. First steps

'Be not afraid of going slowly, be afraid only of standing still.'

Chinese Proverb

Do your research

Before you move, it's advisable to undertake some simple research using the resources mentioned in this book, and by reading blogs and websites.

The government gateway website (https://www.gov.uk) is a starting point for gathering information and to access government services.

- Work advice - Finding work, your workplace rights, government pensions, national minimum pay rates, income tax bands
- Transport - Apply for a UK driving licence, understand the Highway Code
- Education - Apply for student finance, find a school place, get to know the British school curriculum
- Visas & immigration - Arriving in the UK, visa types & detailed guidance
- Citizenship - Register to vote, apply for residency

Initial practicalities

The first few days and weeks of arriving in a new country can be a busy and daunting time.

Here are some steps to take.

- Find somewhere to live. It's a good idea to book somewhere short-term for the first couple of weeks. Once you are in the country you will be in a better position to apply for somewhere for longer.
- Get a National Insurance number. This is required to work and may be printed on the back of your biometric residence permit. Otherwise, you can apply online. Once you have started working you will find the number at the top of your payslip.
- Open a bank account. A bank account will allow you to get paid and avoid costly overseas money transfers. This usually requires you to provide a UK residential address.
- Get a local SIM card for your mobile/cell phone. A local phone will be essential for finding somewhere to live and international calls will add up. These can be bought at an airport when you arrive.

- Check where branches of your bank are located. You may find that your bank doesn't have any branches in the UK but that you can still access its services through a subsidiary.

- Check if your services e.g. pension scheme, insurance have any geographic restrictions.

- Redirect post (mail) from your old address to your new one.

- Update your address as required - insurance, banks, bills, licences. For instance, I had home contents insurance, that if I had tried to claim on, would have been invalid as my address had changed. Equally, you don't want any of your sensitive information going astray.

- Register with a family doctor (General Practitioner / GP) and dentist. The National Health Service (NHS) is used by the majority of residents and offers world leading care. There is usually no need to have any private healthcare or health insurance. It's funded through National Insurance and general tax contributions. It's worth considering the proximity and opening hours of local services.

Orientation

When you first arrive in the UK, I would strongly recommend giving yourself some time to do some sightseeing. In case you aren't already excited about moving, you hopefully will be after seeing some sights and that enthusiasm will really help you to mark off some of the things on your to do list.

My first visit to London was in 2005 when I travelled from Scotland and back on the same day to attend an event. Before my train home I had a few hours free so decided to make the most of being in the capital by taking an open top bus tour. As a young person, I found it a thrilling experience. It's a great way to get your bearings of a place and the live commentaries can be a lot of fun.

Most bus tours are the 'hop on hop off variety', taking an hour to go the whole way around a route. Tickets are usually valid for 24 hours, so if you plan your route can be combined with visiting attractions. Tours are offered with live commentary in English as well as audio guides in other languages.

An alternative to a bus tour is to experience a place at street level by taking a paid or free walking tour. At the street level, you will be able to experience the pulse of the nation; the buildings, the weather, the smells and local conversations. Walking tours provide an immersive experience and allow plenty of opportunities for discussions with your guide. A free walking tour costs nothing to attend and you are encouraged to tip as much as you feel the tour was worth at the end. A tip of £10 to £20 is reasonable.

Improve your English

English may not be your first language so you may wish to improve your understanding. Communicating in English is essential to living in the UK and is assessed as part of visa applications.

Although many languages are spoken by immigrants to the UK, it's unusual to find native Brits that speak other languages fluently. It's not that Brits are lazy, it's just that there are so many English speakers in the world that there can be little incentive to learn another language. The most common second languages that British school kids learn are French, German and Spanish.

If you want to improve your English there are many books, online courses, videos, podcasts and classroom courses that can help. A good place to start if you are currently outside the country is to check out the online resources and courses offered by The British Council, an international charity that promotes Britain and the English language.

5. Finding a place to call home

'There is nothing like staying at home for real comfort.'

Jane Austen (1775-1817), author

Run your own removal service

If you are moving from outside the UK, the cost of shipping your items will depend on where you are travelling from and the number of items you plan to transport. As space is at a premium, you may wish to only transport what you need with you as luggage.

However, if you are planning to settle in the UK for the longer term or have much to move, check out companies accredited by the *FIDI*, the largest global grouping of international moving and relocation companies. It's sensible to take out comprehensive insurance on the move.

From Europe

The cheapest way to move your belonging from the continent is to do so yourself. Providing you or someone you know holds a driving licence and meets the requirements you can hire a van and move your own belongings yourself. Higher insurance costs for younger drivers may mean that companies will place a minimum age restriction on drivers.

Vehicles can be hired from one of the big companies such as *Europcar*, *Enterprise* or *Hertz*. Companies will offer to reduce your insurance excess for an extra fee. Assuming you are comfortable driving and aren't driving for long you will probably not need to do this.

Another extra, they may try to sell you is satellite navigation ('sat nav'). Save your pennies and use your mobile's navigation instead. The *Google Maps* app provided just as good if not better navigation as a premium satellite navigation device. Download maps in advance using Wi-Fi so that you don't need to use data. It is worth investing in a basic phone holder to attach your phone to the dashboard. You might also want a paper 'A to Z style map' as a backup in case your phone battery dies.

If you plan to hire a vehicle several times, you can sign up to one of the car club schemes such as *Zipcar* or *Enterprise Car Club*, whereby vehicles can be hired by the hour. Car clubs are also a cheaper option than having your own car once you have moved. For instance, they can be useful for doing a big food shop or for the odd road trip out of the city.

Packing your belongings up is easy with a set of cardboard packing boxes. Moving sets including packing boxes, bubble wrap and marker pens, can be ordered online.

A word on London

If you are planning to move to London then get ready to downsize. Unless you are in the top one percent (in which case you may be reading the wrong book) if you are moving from just about anywhere that isn't one of a small handful of the world's biggest cities, you will almost certainly have to downsize. Prepare yourself to be shocked at how expensive shoe boxes can be.

According to a recent study[2], the floor area of the average house in the UK is less than any other country in Europe. The average floor area of a new UK home is

---

[2] *Quantifying the extent of space shortages: English dwellings.* Morgan, M. and Cruikshank, H. Building Research & Information, 2014.
http://www.tandfonline.com/doi/full/10.1080/09613218.2014.92 2271

just 76 m^2, compared to 109.2 m^2 in Germany and 137 m^2 in Denmark. Accommodation in London is the least spacious in the UK, often reflecting that houses have been split into flats.

To help with downsizing you may want to reduce the amount of stuff you own. There are many benefits of taking a minimalistic mindset and it can be said that we don't own stuff, stuff owns us. We all want to live in comfort but that doesn't mean you need to be surrounded by more than you need to be comfortable.

You might have an extensive wardrobe, book or record collection proudly displayed in your living room back home. But the reality is that your new pad may not even have a living room. It's long been common for landlords to convert a living room into another bedroom to increase their rental yield.

Choosing a country

You may be wondering, wait how do I decide which country to move to, after all, isn't the UK also a country? Yes, the UK is a country, but remember it is also made up of four countries; England, Wales, Scotland and Northern Ireland (the Home Nations).

Well, don't worry too much about which country within the UK you want to move to. You can always move within the country later. It's a relatively small island and easy to get around.

If I had to place a bet, I would place a tenner that you probably want to move to London in the south-east of England. But don't rule out the other bits above it. If you are looking for somewhere lively there are plenty of big cities to consider including Manchester, Birmingham, Newcastle, Cardiff, Belfast and Glasgow.

As a Scot that adores their home nation, I will try not to be too biased towards it. But in my opinion, if you can choose anywhere in the UK, I would suggest Edinburgh as a great all-round city with buckets of culture, a thriving economy and a high quality of living. Culture is in plentiful supply with the city hosting the world's largest arts festival every August. The only downside is that Scotland tends to be a bit colder and wetter than the south of England, where invariably most will gravitate towards.

Choosing an area

A good indication of an area to avoid when weighing up where to live is whether you have previously heard of it. Chances are the places you have heard of before through film or TV are going to be completely outside of your price range.

For instance, don't expect to be living in a west end London mansion e.g. *Made in Chelsea* or a Yorkshire country estate e.g. *Downton Abbey*. These places are highly desirable and most likely beyond your budget, so you may need to adjust your expectations.

A good starting point for getting to know an area's geography better is to simply lay out a large paper map or use online maps and just spend some time familiarising yourself with the layout, the names and scale of the country. This understanding will be essential when arranging house viewings. Viewings are often arranged quickly and may provide little time for deciding on taking a place.

There is no right area to consider when deciding where to live. You probably want to find a balance between some of the following aspects.

- Commute cost and distance to work, college or university
- Proximity to friends, family and places you will want to visit
- Accommodation you will enjoy that is within your budget
- Local amenities such as restaurants, cafes, supermarkets and parks

It is worth considering both the time and monetary cost of finding a place to live. It's useful to obtain a travel card if you are hopping around town viewing different properties as making multiple single journeys can quickly add up.

Finally, The Sunday Times Best Places to Live 2018 guide[3] compared quality of life across the UK. Here are the regional winners.

South East - Berkhamsted, Hertfordshire

East - Chelmsford, Essex

Midlands - Shipston-on-Stour, Warwickshire

3 The Sunday Times. https://www.thetimes.co.uk/article/best-places-to-live-sunday-times-3qkwjnvrm

London - Bermondsey

North West - Altrincham, Greater Manchester

South West - Frome, Somerset

North East - Tynemouth, Northumberland

Wales - Mumbles, Swansea

Scotland - Melrose, Scottish Borders

Northern Ireland - Ballyhackamore, Belfast

Accommodation costs

Chances are if you are reading this book, you are planning to rent but even if you can afford to buy you probably will have a stretched disposable income and will benefit from reducing your cost of living. The average property price in the UK is around £225,000, with monthly mortgage payments typically around £800 per month.

Renters typically stay in shared accommodation either houses (house-shares) or apartments/flats (flat-shares).

In London, the high cost of accommodation means it is unusual for a single person to live in a 1 bedroom flat, with studios available for those who want more privacy. It's common for houses to be subdivided into multiple flats or studios with shared entrances. Outside of London, it is usually affordable for a single person to rent a 1 bedroom flat.

Over recent years, a combination of factors has led to large year-on-year rises in rents in many areas of the UK. These include increasing property prices, a booming buy to let mortgage market and a growing economy. However, restrictions on the buy to let market, weaker economic growth and political upheaval have led to decreasing rents and property prices.

Here are some tips for finding better value accommodation.

- Explore the suburbs. Suburban areas tend to have lower cost housing and offer the potential for a higher quality of living compared to city centres. In some cities, the cost can relate to different travel zones. In London, accommodation in zones 2 or 3 will be less than zone 1.
- Keep an open mind. Consider areas that may not be immediately obvious.
- Look for places further away from train stations that are still well-connected by bus. Most places will have

a good bus route within walking distance. Check how frequent services run if you need to change.

- Ex-council flats may not be appealing from the outside but can be more spacious than other options. They are a popular choice among young professionals.
- If you can do without large communal areas, the rental price will reduce. Many landlords have converted living rooms into bedrooms and the main living space is now the kitchen. Larger kitchens with ample space can fit in a table and some chairs.

Finding places to stay

By far the best method of finding places to stay is to ask people you already know if they have a spare room or if they know someone who does. Not only is this a free, low-stress approach but you also are also more likely to find compatible housemates.

Viewing properties online before your move is a great first step, but you will want to view properties in person to understand the market and to ensure you really are happy to stay there. This particularly applies if you want a room in a shared house, so will want to ensure you get on with the other housemates. Wide angle photos taken by the letting agency can be deceptive, rooms may be smaller than they appear online.

In recent years, there has been a rise in pre-booked online accommodation turning out to be a scam, so don't take the risk. For peace of mind, book accommodation in a hotel or *Airbnb* for a few nights to get you settled in, then once on the ground you can start viewings.

Viewings can be arranged through a letting/estate agent or directly through a landlord. Often agents can be pushy but don't rush into making a decision unless you are completely happy with your decision. You will have to live in the property after all.

For popular rental properties, open viewings are common, where viewings will be scheduled for 2-3 hours at a time with an agent to hand to answer questions. This type of open viewing often makes renters nervous as they assume, they will have to move fast if they wish to take it. This is often the case in the big cities, unfortunately, so it is sensible to know what's on your wish list and if you are just browsing or seriously looking.

It's worth doing research online before you attend the viewing so that you can go beyond the basic facts such as how many rooms it has and how much it costs, to asking questions such as what type of heating system is fitted or asking the current residents how noisy the neighbours are.

Give yourself enough time to see a range of properties and know when you have seen enough places to make a sensible decision.

During your property search, be financially prepared to commit to a property straight away. Landlords can legally ask for up to two months' rent as a deposit plus there will be a variable amount required for reference and administrative fees. Landlords are required to put tenant deposits into a government-based tenancy deposit scheme. If there is a dispute over the deposit, it will be held in the scheme until the dispute is settled.

It's common for tenants to move addresses regularly as leases end or tenants finding a better place to stay. Additionally, it worth remembering there is a good chance that the first place you find to live will not be your forever home, even if you wished to stay there for the long-term. Landlords may decide to sell up, flatmates may decide to move out or you may decide you want to move in with your significant other.

Accommodation resources

- *SpareRoom* - Search to find an existing house/flat shares. Sign up to their Early Bird service for instant messaging to any posting. The website has some tools to help find an area by commute time, travel zone or Tube line.

- *EasyRoommate* - Search for existing house/flat shares. Like *SpareRoom*, also offers a premium service that offers wider searching abilities.

- *Movebubble* - Search for existing house/flat shares. Popular mobile app.

- *OpenRent* - Skip the letting agency and rent directly from the landlord to reduce your upfront costs. It is free to search and becoming increasingly popular.

- *Roomi* - Listings site and mobile app. Provides some useful comparison stats.

- *GumTree* - Popular listings site for just about everything including a dedicated rentals board. Also, useful when selling stuff before moving.

- Letting/estate agencies - If you have an area in mind it is worth visiting the high street where there are likely to be a few agents. Browse the window ads and speak to a few agents. Once you have told an agent you are interested in the area, they will take your details and get in contact as new properties come on the market. It's also useful to speak to local agents about the characteristics of the local area such as typical renters/buyers, local things to do and typical costs.

- *Rightmove & Zoopla* - Large online directories that advertise whole properties to rent, many useful search tools such as map and public transport searches. Mobile apps are useful for arranging appointments on the move.

- *Purple Bricks* - Online estate agent that sells for a fixed fee, without taking a commission. The increasingly popular business model may become a major challenger to the traditional estate agent.

- *Tepilo* - Another online estate agent that sells for a fixed fee, without taking a commission.

Finally, remember it's not just a property you are looking for, to some extent you are also looking for a good landlord. Most landlords will, of course, meet all their duties and treat you well. Recommendations and accreditation by the *UK Landlord Accreditation Scheme* or the *National Landlord Association* can help.

It's also important to read the lease agreement and thoroughly check any inventory before you move in. You may wish to take photos after you move in to help provide evidence for any later discussions.

Furnishing your home

Your new place may come furnished, unfurnished or even part-furnished. Even if it is furnished you may not like what you have and wish to replace or update it. Most rental properties in the lower to mid-range will come furnished while many rental properties at the higher end will come unfurnished. A furnished room will typically include a double bed, chest of drawers, table/desk and a chair.

The most common place to buy starter furniture is IKEA, the low-cost Swedish flatpack furniture store. IKEA furniture is very common in rental properties and most towns have an IKEA store within easy reach. Items can be home delivered for a fee but this will not include assembly, which will inevitably take much longer than you expect. Assembling furniture can be tiring and I always require a couple of breaks to get through the ordeal.

If you are looking for furniture it is worth checking *Freecycle*. It is an excellent resource for finding just about anything that someone else no longer finds useful. The way it works is that user who wants to get rid of their stuff advertise it on a group list and if you are a member of that list you get an email detailing what is available. Much of what is offered is lower quality but sometimes you just need some shelves or a juicer and the person offering those items may be moving and doesn't want the hassle of transporting them.

Be suspicious of *Freecycle* listings that contain a description but don't contain any photos. Descriptions can be misleading and what you and the owner consider a fair consider may differ. If you turn up and don't like what you see then you are under no obligation to take the items. You can politely walk away.

Consider that larger items may require a vehicle to transport them home. A willing taxi driver may be an easier way to transport large items than hiring a vehicle.

Forever homes

This book is primarily focused on moving to the UK in the here and now. However, in the longer term, you may wish to find a forever home. Or at least a home you want to live in for the foreseeable future.

For many young Britons, the UK is simply too expensive to buy a property without family help. London is particularly challenging, with a record number of 30-somethings leaving the capital for either commuter-friendly towns or other big English cities such as Birmingham or Manchester. However, if you are interested in settling here longer you may wish to research getting on the property ladder.

The property ladder is the somewhat antiquated concept that buying a home is like climbing a ladder. You start at the bottom with a smaller property and use the equity you build up along with any increase in property prices to buy a larger, more expensive property.

Currently, UK property prices, particularly at the upper end are falling and Brexit may dampen prices further. However, in the longer-term prices are unlikely to fall (see crystal ball prediction) so this may be a good time to buy a UK property.

A combination of low interest rates and a reduction in property purchases due to restrictions on the buy to let market have led it to be an attractive time to buy a property. That is if you can afford the deposit. Currently, you can buy with as little as a 5% deposit but for the average UK property, this can still be as much as 5-20K.

If you don't mind taking on a project you may wish to consider an auction property. Auction properties are typically properties that have resulted from bankruptcy and are often in poor condition. Interested parties attend an auction and bid on their preferred property, with the highest offer securing the keys.

Another affordable way to get onto the first rung of the property ladder is through shared ownership, whereby you buy a proportion of a property and pay an affordable rent on the remainder you don't own. Rent increases are controlled by legislation. Shared ownership is primarily designed for those who can afford a monthly mortgage payment but can't save a large enough deposit to buy a property outright. It is restricted to first time buyers and priority is often given to those who live or work locally to the property.

6. Working in the UK

'I suppose I've created an atmosphere where I'm a friend first and a boss second. Probably an entertainer third.'

David Brent, boss

Working scene

There is, of course, no typical work week but the average salaried UK office worker will work a 37-hour week. This usually equates to 9 am to 5 pm with a 30 minutes lunch break or 9 am to 5.30 pm with a one-hour lunch break. Some organisations finish earlier on a Friday.

It's increasingly common for employers to offer flexible working, whereby staff can agree to different working hours to fit around commutes, childcare, dentist appointments, other activities or responsibilities.

Based on a typical five-day work week, staff are entitled to at least 28 days paid leave per year. An employer can include 8 public holidays (also known as Bank Holidays) within this 28-day entitlement, but many do not. Public holidays include New Year's Day (1st January), Good Friday, Easter Monday, Early May Bank Holiday, Spring

Bank Holiday, Summer Bank Holiday, Christmas Day (25th December) and Boxing Day (26th December).

In addition to the standard paid leave and public holidays, there are other types of leave including sick leave when an individual is unable to work because they are ill and parental leave for new parents.

Finding a job in the UK

Finding a job in the UK will depend on the sector you wish to work in and your level of experience. The UK has a good rate of employment with the unemployment rate currently at 4.3%[4].

There are a few ways to find a job

- Register with a recruitment agency and let them find a job for you. There are hundreds of agencies, many focused-on specialist sectors that can provide tailored industry advice. Be aware that once

---

[43] *Statistical Bulletin: UK Labour Market: March 2018*. Office for National Statistics.

https://www.ons.gov.uk/employmentandlabourmarket/peoplein work/employmentandemployeetypes/bulletins/uklabourmarket/ march2018 registered you could be inundated with emails and calls. Tell them once you have secured a position.

- Apply directly for a vacancy. The role might be advertised on a company's website or a jobs site.
- Ask any friends or contacts who work in your industry if they can get you a job. It's said that around half of all jobs are never advertised and it is certainly easier for an employer to acquire a new member of staff through an employee recommendation. Many companies have referral schemes that reward employees for recruiting a new colleague.
- Send speculative applications to companies you would like to work for. If the company likes the sound of you, they might just create a position.

Recruitment agencies

- Adecco
- Blue Arrow
- Hays
- Michael Page

Online jobs boards

- *Indeed* - Extensive range of roles

- *Jobsite* - Extensive range of roles
- *Monster* - Includes useful careers advice
- *Reed* - Extensive range of roles
- *Universal Jobmatch* - Job centre roles

Most workers on a salary get paid monthly into a bank account. This contrasts with North America and other places in the world where it is more common to be paid weekly or fortnightly. British staff paid by the hour are usually paid weekly. Casual workers may be paid cash in hand but employers must still pay Income Tax and National Insurance.

It is important to check your payslip carefully when you start a new job, to ensure you aren't being deducted more than you ought to be. Secondly, while it can be painful to see so much being taken off your income, particularly if you have moved from a country with lower taxation, an understanding of the numbers can help to soothe the pain.

Deductions

- Income Tax - Largest deduction and used for general government spending. Check you are on the right tax code when you start a new job (including internal moves).

- National Insurance - Contributions towards the NHS, state pensions, maternity cover and other benefits. You can log into the UK government website to find out how many years you have contributed so far and how many you need to before you are eligible for your state pension.
- Student loan contributions - Usually for studies undertaken in the UK
- Pension contributions - Mandatory employee auto-enrolment
- Miscellaneous - Travel card, cycle to work contributions, adjustments

Income Tax

Most workers pay income tax through their employer, through the Pay As Your Earn (PAYE) system, where income tax is taken off wages by an employer and paid directly to the government. If you are self-employed you need to pay your own tax. The government gateway site (https://www.gov.uk) can provide guidance.

Note, that the exact amount of income tax you pay will also depend on employee benefits. For instance, if you have a company car.

The exact tax you will pay will largely depend on your pay. Income tax is paid on earnings above the *Personal Allowance*, currently set at £12,500 per year and has increased considerably in recent years. The *Personal Allowance* may be higher if you claim the *Marriage Allowance* or *Blind Person's Allowance* but is smaller if your income is above £100,000.

It's important to make sure you are on the right tax code. If you are on the wrong tax code, for instance, the emergency tax code BR, you will receive no tax-free personal allowance so will pay more tax. Everything you earn will be taxed at the basic rate of 20%, so could result in hundreds of more pounds being deducted each month.

Let the *HMRC* (Her Majesty's Revenue and Customs) know straight away to ensure that you get put on the right tax code as soon as possible and to apply for a tax refund (known as a tax rebate). If you have overpaid tax it will be refunded but this may not be straight away.

Tax Relief

Tax relief is a reduction in tax or a tax refund. You may be eligible for tax relief when you use your own money for travel or to buy other things you require for work.

You can claim tax relief on things that are just used for work, that aren't used in your personal time. It's important to keep records and claim within four years of the end of the tax year that you spent the money.

Examples of what can be claimed

- Work uniforms
- Professional development
- Vehicle mileage
- Pensions

Pensions

Pensions are a type of savings account for your retirement, to provide a source of income when you are no longer working. There are, generally speaking, two types of pension available in the UK, the state pension and a private pension.

State Pension

The State Pension is the pension provided by the UK government. It is funded through National Insurance contributions. It is paid to British nationals and non-British nationals working in the UK.

To be eligible for the state pension you need to have made between 10 and 30 qualifying years of national insurance contributions or credits. The lowest amount is given for 10 qualifying years and this increases to the full state pension with 30 qualifying years. You can check how many years you have on your record through the government gateway website.

If you have worked part-time or have periods of unemployment it is worth checking if you acquired a qualifying year or not. The government tax body, the HMRC allows individuals to make top-up payments to convert a non-qualifying year into a qualifying year in some cases.

Private Pensions

Private pensions are usually workplace pensions that are organised by the employer but managed by a private pension provider. Employees are often auto-enrolled into a pension scheme and have to opt-out if they decide they don't want to be part of it. Contributions are typically a percentage of an employee's salary that is deducted from their pay and paid directly into the pension fund (or pot).

The employer will commonly also make a contribution to the pension pot, often matching the employee's contribution percentage. As an employee's salary increases, the contributions will increase as the percentage equate to a larger sum. In many organisations, the employer sets the minimum contribution percentages for different salary levels.

In addition to workplace pensions, an individual may set up their own private pension, also known as a personal pension. A private pension is one that is organised by the individual with no state or employer contributions.

The amount provided by a private pension depends on the contributions made during its lifetime. Higher contributions over a long period of time will provide a more generous pension than smaller contributions over a shorter time period.

Unlike the state pension, there is no cap on the amount that can be paid out, meaning a private pension could provide a significant part of your retirement income. Taxes may apply to very large pension pots or when money is withdrawn.

Tax relief at the basic rate is given on all private pension contributions. For instance, a payment of £50 would gain £10 relief, making the total contribution £60.

Top tips

- Maximise your monthly contributions. The contribution percentage set by an employer in a workplace pension is often quite low, for instance, three or four percent. By increasing this percentage, you can increase the size of your pension pot faster. Due to the magic of compound interest, it's best to pay in more sooner, rather than waiting for the years before retirement when contributions would have to be larger to save the same amount.
- Manage your private pensions online. Pension providers offer a service similar to online banking where customers can login to view transactions, check investment growth and make ad-hoc payments. Forecasting tools are available to project likely pension pot sizes and the monthly pay out.
- Keep track of pensions when you change job. Currently, when an employee changes job the

contributions will cease and the new employer will enrol you in their scheme. In the context of people changing role every few years, this is a far from an ideal system. In this situation, the funds from an old pension scheme can be transferred to a new pension scheme. It is more profitable to have one large pension pot than several small ones. Another option is to continue making personal contributions to the old scheme, in the form of a standing order.

7. Education, Education, Education

'Our top priority was, is and always will be education, education, education. To overcome decades of neglect and make Britain a learning society, developing the talents and raising the ambitions of all our young people.'

Tony Blair (1953-), British Prime Minister

Schools

The school system is divided into pre-school, primary and secondary. Pre-school is also known as nursery or kindergarten provides early education and childcare prior to compulsory education.

Schooling is compulsory between the ages of 5 and 16 across the UK. In England, you must remain in some type of education or training until the age of 18. Education is devolved in Scotland, Wales and Northern Ireland means the rules are slightly different. For instance, there are different curriculums and different qualifications.

Children are generally grouped with others of around the same age. The first year of primary school in England & Wales is referred to as the reception year, while primary schools in Scotland and Northern Ireland refer to the same year as primary or level 1.

School years across most of the UK refer to the number of years from the start of primary school. In England & Wales primary school runs between years 1 to 6, secondary school runs between years 7 to 13. In Northern Ireland primary school runs between years 1 to 7 and secondary school refers to years 8 to 14. In Scotland primary school refers to primary 1 to primary 7 and secondary schools refers to secondary year 1 to secondary year 6.

Types of schools

- State - the majority of schools, run by local councils and follow a national curriculum. The majority are non-selective, where students are not admitted based on some sort of admissions criteria, usually academic. State schools that are non-selective in England and Wales are also known as Comprehensive Schools.
- Faith - follow the national curriculum but focus on a particular religion.

- Grammar - selective state schools in England & Wales that select using the '11-plus' exam.
- Academies & Free Schools - state schools that are allowed more freedom over admissions, curriculum and timetables.
- Integrated schools - a type of state school in Northern Ireland that brings together different religions.
- Independent - private schools funded by paying school fees. Also known as public schools in England & Wales.

Types of qualifications

England, Wales, Northern Ireland

- GCSEs - Years 10 & 11 (England & Wales), Years 11 & 12 (N. Ireland)
- A Levels - Years 12 & 13 (England & Wales), Years 13 & 14 (N. Ireland)

Scotland

- National 4/5s - S4 to S6
- Highers / Advanced Highers - S5 to S6

Choosing a school

To find out generally about local schools, the best place to start is to look at the council website. The website can advise about the admission criteria for the schools you are interested in and to apply for places in schools in other areas.

Schools typically have a catchment area, a defined geographic area that gives priority to children living within the catchment.

You can find out more about a school by visiting the school. Most schools arrange Open Days for prospective parents to see the buildings and meet the staff.

You can also read about the school's standards using the appropriate national agency to find school inspection reports. The academic performance of students, for instance, how many students achieve a certain grade can be found using school league tables.

Further education

Further education refers to education following the completion of secondary school but not including graduate and postgraduate courses. Most further education establishments are referred to as colleges. This is not to be confused with the North American use of the word college. The term college can also be used to refer to different departments in a university.

Colleges offer a range of courses from basic maths and English to Higher National Diplomas (HNDs).

Universities

Universities in the UK provide Higher Education, courses at the undergraduate and postgraduate level. The UK has a large number of universities that teach a wide range of subjects.

The UK has some of the best performing research universities in the world. Many of these are in the Russell Group, an elite group of older universities including the world leading Oxford and Cambridge universities.

Universities are funded through a mixture of sources including students paying tuition fees, government funding, endowments and business. Students pay tuition fees to study in England, Wales and Northern Ireland. Students in Scotland do not have to pay tuition fees.

8. Getting around

'I grew up in Zimbabwe in Southern Africa, and I moved to London when I was 17. And I started commuting and, actually, to go to college. And I used to really enjoy that part of my journey where the - it was actually a Tube train, but it was overground, and it went right past the backs of people's houses, and I could actually see right in.'

Paula Hawkins (1972-), author

Transport scene

Britain has a developed public transport network in urban areas although fares can be expensive. Rural areas have fewer public transport options and the use of a car can be more of a necessity.

Many cities have highly integrated public transport networks with passengers able to switch seamlessly between trains, trams, subways and buses. Smart travel cards can increasingly be used to pay for journeys.

Adult fares are charged for those aged 18 and over. Concessions - students, children and those aged over 60 pay a reduced price. Small children travel for free.

Driving in the UK can be expensive, particularly parking and insurance but there are many tips and tricks to help reduce the cost.

Underground services

There is an extensive underground service in London and small underground networks in Newcastle and Glasgow. In London, the transport network is divided into a series of zones. Zone 1 is broadly central London with increasing numbers leading to outer London.

Night services

Night services are common across many transport networks, particularly bus services in urban areas. London recently launched night services across much of the tube and overground services, with fares considered off-peak.

Accessibility

The transport network is becoming more accessible to all travellers.

That said, it is disappointing that in London most Tube stations still don't have step-free access despite the millions of passengers who use the service every day.

- Step-free access. Step-free access is defined as lifts, escalators or ramps. All buses have a dedicated wheelchair space and offer ramp access. In London, a quarter of Tube stations, half of the overground stations and all DLR stations have step-free access.

- Dedicated seating onboard. Priority seating is provided for passengers that are less able to stand is available on all buses, Tubes, trains and trams. Passengers who require a seat can order a free badge to alert other passengers. Other passengers should be aware they are likely to be asked to move if they take priority seating, particularly on a busy service.

Commuting

Commuting is the act of getting from home to work and back again. A recent study[5] examined the relationship

[5] *The Commuting and Wellbeing Study.* Changing Travel Behaviours, 2017. https://travelbehaviour.com/outputs-commuting-wellbeing

between wellbeing and commuting. It found that every extra minute spent commuting reduces job satisfaction, reduces leisure time satisfaction, increases stress and reduces mental health. However, it did also find that active commuting, such as walking and cycling to work increase wellbeing and that taking longer train journeys are less strenuous than shorter journeys.

Top commuter tips

- Plan your commute - Check the best route for your journey. The fastest, cheapest or most comfortable commute may not be the most obvious.

- Test drive your new commute - Before you move to a new job or home, it's worth trying a new commute to see how you find it. Whether it is better or worse than another commute will be down to personal preference.

- Keep entertained - Free newspapers and magazines are given away at stations and often left on seats. When I get bored on a journey, I walk down a carriage to find a paper. Music, podcasts and audiobooks are also a great way to pass the time.

- Stay cool - Trains and buses can get very hot, particularly in summer so it worth layering up so you can cool down easily. Carrying water and some emergency snacks are helpful for the inevitable delays.

Plan your route

Planning the fastest, most comfortable or cheapest route from A to B takes time. For most people, the cost is the most important factor as travel can be a sizeable chunk of your expenses.

You can potentially save money by avoiding certain travel zones or favouring cheaper forms of transport. Taking the train or underground will typically be faster but more expensive than taking the bus, cycling or walking.

The most comprehensive transport planning tool is probably *Google Maps*, that can be used for comparing car, public transport and walking options. An alternative is the *Traveline* website.

For public transport, the mobile app *Citymapper* is handy and provides a more creative set of options. It currently has coverage in Birmingham, London, Manchester, with more cities planned.

Travel cards

Smart travel cards used to pay for public transport are becoming more common. With a smart card, you tap on a reader at the start of your journey and sometimes at the end.

Oyster is *Transport for London's* smart card and is the most popular payment method. Even if you aren't based in London you are likely to visit so it is worth being aware of how they work. New *Oyster* cards can be purchased from ticket offices and require a £5 refundable deposit. *Oyster* cards can hold pay as you go credit, travel cards and Bus & Tram passes.

Top Oyster tips

- On-peak fares apply Monday to Friday 06.30-09.30 and 16.00-19.00, excluding public holidays. Off-peak fares apply at other times and if you travel from a station outside Zone 1 to a station in Zone 1 between 16:00 and 19:00, Mondays to Friday.
- Check the cost before you travel. The Transport for London website has a costings tool to make sure you know what you will pay. This is useful to help compare the cost of travelling pay as you go versus

using a travel card. Ticket barriers display the charge at the end of a journey.

- Fares are capped at a daily maximum for pay as you go fares.

- Register your card online to top-up, check your balance and in case it is lost or stolen. A mobile app is also available. Cards must be registered in order to apply for refunds, although this can be done after it is purchased.

- Remember to top-up your Oyster card before you use it. If you go over your balance you will go into negative money which still allows you to exit a station so you can top-up.

- Contactless payments (Apple Pay, Android Pay, contactless credit cards) use pay as you go.

- Pay as you go fares are charged if you don't have a travel card. If you have a travel card and credit on your Oyster it will use the travel card, assuming it covers the journey. If the travel card only covers part of your journey, the remaining amount will be debited from the card's balance.

- When exiting a station, to pay the correct fare, it is important to 'tap out' using your *Oyster* at the ticket barrier. In most cases it won't be possible to leave without tapping out, however, gates are often opened to alleviate passenger flows. At some stations, for instance, some DLR stations there are no ticket barriers.

- Travel cards can be added to an *Oyster* card and can be daily, weekly, monthly or annual. They can cover one or more travel zones, for instance just zone 1 or zones 2 to 4. Travel cards can be purchased at stations or online. It's worth remembering that if you buy a card and it is no longer needed, you can get it refunded minus a small administrative charge.

It's worth taking some time to consider the right travel card for you.

- How often you travel for work. If you plan to work from home or work part-time it may be cheaper to pay as you go rather than buying a weekly card.
- How often you travel in your free time. If you regularly go into the city centre in your free time, then the travel card may cover this.
- The zones the card is needed for. In London avoid zone 1 if you can, as all travel cards are substantially cheaper if they exclude it. For example, if you live in zone 4 and commute into zone 2 the quickest route

may be to travel through zone 1 but if you can accept a longer journey then you might just save a small fortune.

It will usually be cheaper to use a weekly or monthly card than paying as you go. While it is tempting to go for the immediate convenience of tapping your debit card in and out it soon adds up.

If you travel frequently then purchasing an annual travel card could save you money over buying monthly, weekly or pay as you go travel. Another reason to buy an annual card is to delay the annual price increases. Price inflation means the cost of a travel card usually increases by a few percent each January. Buying an annual travel card will lock in the cost for the time remaining on the card, meaning you could be paying the previous year's prices well into the following year.

A potential reason you may be put off buying a season ticket is that you may feel it ties you into a specific route when you may want to move home or work in the next year. But you should be able to get a refund as long as there is a specified amount of time remaining on the card. It's probably sensible to check before the refund terms before you sign up.

If you know with confidence you aren't going to move or change job locations out with the specified zones then buying a standard annual travel card is a big saving over monthly cards, even with holidays factored in. Many employers offer to buy the cost of a travel card upfront for you and then a monthly payment is taken from your salary at the end of the month.

Purchasing an annual season ticket includes a *Gold Card* which gives you 1/3 off national rail journeys, which is a potentially huge saving. The *Gold Card* gives more flexibility that other national rail cards such as Two Together.

Taking the train is more affordable if you have a national rail card.

Travel cards with 1/3 off

- Gold Card - Free to annual season ticket holders, technically only applies to south England but can still use to buy tickets to areas outside the area.
- Two Together - For two adults travelling together, usually used by couples.

- 16-25 / Student - 1 and 3-year options are available. Passengers can purchase or renew a 1-year card until the day before their 26th birthday and can buy/renew a 3-year card until the day before their 24th birthday. By maximising the time on the 3-year card it can be used until the day before your 26th birthday. This is an incredible saving from simply knowing how the rules work.
- Senior - For those aged over 60.
- Disabled Persons - For two people, such as a disabled person and companion.

Other travel cards

- Family & Friends - Kids get 60% off tickets, no adult savings.

It is important to remember to travel with your railcard whenever you have booked using the card. If you forget it you may be charged the full price, but you can now get this difference refunded later.

Tip! Avoid buying a new travel card during the busy Monday morning rush hour. You can avoid the queues by topping up online or using the app.

Automobiles

Owning a car can get very expensive, particularly the cost of parking and car insurance. In most areas' residents' parking is provided on-street spots and a permit will need to be obtained through the council's parking website.

The cheapest car insurance can be obtained by looking around through a price comparison site such as *GoCompare* or *CompareTheMarket*. Insurers such as *Bell* may give a discount if you can demonstrate you are a careful driver through fitting a recording box over a few months.

The reputation of diesel cars has taken a battering recently due to air pollution concerns and sales have sharply declined.

Use your feet

Getting around on foot is both incredibly convenient and easy, particularly in town and city centres.

Tip! *Travel maps are not geographically accurate. In other words, the space between stations on a map is not proportional to distance on the ground.*

Cycle hire schemes

The UK has a growing number of cycle hire schemes. The most notable is in London. Launched in 2010 under Mayor Boris Johnson and the bikes were referred to as *'Boris Bikes'*. Since then the scheme has grown and there are currently more than 11,500 bikes across 750 docking stations.

The scheme is currently sponsored by the bank *Santander* and is called the *Santander Cycle Hire Scheme*. Docking stations are located across central London and some surrounding areas with many situated outside transport links and major attractions, making them ideal for getting around.

As the first 30 minutes are free, if you can make it to another docking station within this time you only need to pay the daily rental charge (currently set at £2). In theory, you can ride multiple times within a 24-hour period so long as you keep within this interval.

If you use the scheme on a regular basis, for instance as part of your commute, it is worth taking out an annual membership (currently £90) as this will allow you to ride as much as you wish. Membership includes a special key for faster access. A potential advantage of the scheme over using your own bike are the docking stations, as you don't need to worry about where to park.

Santander Cycles are relatively large and clunky so don't expect to be the envy of the road or set any speed records but these characteristics also gives them a little more stability. Bikes are fitted with *Blazer laser lights* that illuminate the road in front to let other users know of your presence.

Getting your own cycle is more cost effective however as after you've paid for the bike your costs should be minimal if you can learn some simple maintenance. Additionally, the cycle hire scheme is only feasible if a journey is within proximity to a docking station.

If you decide you want to cycle on a regular basis for work or leisure you will probably want to get your own set of wheels.

Buying a new bike can be expensive but buying second-hand will save a lot. In all second-hand cases, you should make sure that the bike hasn't stolen by buying from a reputable source. Folding bikes are expensive but may be your only option if you need to combine your cycle with the Tube network.

Major improvements have been made to cycle safety over recent years and the number of cyclists has soared. It is worth remembering however that towns and cities have significant road traffic and cyclists should always take care to follow the Highway Code and keep safety in mind for all road users. Always wear a helmet, ensure you have front and rear lights and high visibility clothing.

Taxis

The black cab is a British icon and everyone should take one for the experience. They are spacious, comfortable and you will often have engaging conversations with your driver.

The cheapest taxis are usually private hire vehicles (also known as mini cabs). These either operate independently or part of a scheme such as *Uber*. Taxis can be ordered using an app, on the phone or of course by hailing one down on the street.

Uber is increasingly taking over the taxi space due to its low-cost and convenience. To get started with *Uber* simply download the mobile app and register your details. First rides are often free and you can now even carpool with other passengers.

Uber taxis are very common so usually, don't need to be booked in advance. However, they can now be pre-booked for peace of mind. The app uses your location as the starting point and users specify their destination. The app then sends out a call for a nearby driver. *CityMapper* can also estimate the cost.

It's worth remembering that an *Uber* taxi will charge a penalty if you cancel your booked car after more than 5 minutes.

Planes

As air travel has grown in popularity, greater competition between providers has meant that airlines have considered new ways to reduce ticket costs. As a traveller, it is worth making sure you are aware of the extra costs that you may incur.

- Food & drink - The flight may offer complimentary snacks and drinks but not a full meal, even if it is a long flight. Food & drink can be purchase onboard or ordered in advance in some cases but you may wish to grab a sandwich in the departure lounge.

- Entertainment- There may be a cost to access the inflight entertainment or to hire a device. Streaming services using onboard Wi-Fi are becoming more common.

- Check-in baggage - Rules will vary by airline but for short haul flights, there is usually a charge for checking in a bag. To maximise your cabin baggage, consider buying a specially designed cabin bag that maximises storage space.

- Choosing a seat - There is often a surcharge to choose where you wish to sit.

- Booking fees - Look out for credit card, phone line and other fees. Booking with a debit card will often be free but you may not have the same cover if the airline goes bust or doesn't deliver what is promised.

Travelling to Europe

Continental Europe is accessible by train through the Channel Tunnel on the *Eurostar* and you will lower your carbon footprint if you take the train instead of flying. The *Seat 61* website offers extensive information on planning your train travel from the UK to just about anywhere. It is so-called as the author prefers sitting in seat number 61 when travelling first class from the UK to Paris to ensure a window seat.

If you are planning to travel by train quite a bit outside of the UK it is worth getting a rail pass. Rail passes allow a certain number of days of travel during a chosen time frame. They are available for specific countries, several bordering countries or for extensive travel. Travellers aged 12-27 are classed as Youth travellers and save 20%.

Travelling from the UK to Europe by coach can be a cheaper way to travel if you can tolerate a long journey. It is possible to get a coach from the UK to Paris, Berlin or many other places in Europe for very little money.

Coaches usually leave from Victoria Coach Station in London.

Healthy travelling and insurance

If you are ordinarily resident in Britain and travelling to Europe, it is recommended you apply for a *European Health Insurance Card (EHIC)*. The card provides access to state health care and treatment of pre-existing conditions, during a temporary stay in the European Economic Area (EEA) and Switzerland. The *EHIC* doesn't guarantee healthcare free at the point of use, as you may be used to in the UK, but it ensures you pay what a local would.

If you are travelling outside of Europe, it is highly recommended and indeed for some visas, it is mandatory, to purchase travel insurance. If you don't have travel insurance and require medical assistance you may be required to pay hundreds or even thousands of pounds out of pocket. In that respect, taking out travel insurance is the cheapest way to travel.

Travel insurance tips

- Check for existing cover - Some bank accounts include travel insurance, but this should not be confused with travel accident insurance. Additionally, check if the travel insurance you previously purchased is still valid.
- Look around - Price comparison sites can quickly compare costs for where you are going, length of stay, the number of people and specialist cover such as winter sports.
- Review what's included - A cheaper level of cover may be all you need for a short trip.

In addition to taking out travel insurance, it is prudent to check if you need travel vaccinations. Advice on health matters including vaccinations is available on the Foreign Office website. The cost of vaccinations will depend on what you need and whether you get them on the NHS or not.

9. Everyday practicalities

'They say, if money goes before, all ways do lie open.'

William Shakespeare (1564-1616), playwright

Voting

The nation holds elections to elect representatives for parliament, local authorities and until recently the EU parliament. In addition, a large number of cities in England and Wales have directly elected mayors. Scotland has its' own parliament, Wales Assembly members and Northern Ireland Executive. No elections are held for the House of Lords.

In addition to regular elections, the UK has also hosted several one-off votes including the EU Referendum in 2016, Scotland Independence Referendum in 2014 and a snap UK General Election in 2017.

It is important to register to vote in advance of an election.

Eligibility to vote of non-British nationals varies by election.

- General elections - includes Irish and qualifying Commonwealth Citizens.

- Local elections - includes EU nationals and qualifying Commonwealth Citizens.

The Beeb

This book wouldn't be complete without mentioning the BBC (British Broadcasting Corporation). The BBC is a British public services broadcaster that operates national and regional TV and radio services. It is the world's oldest national broadcasting organisation having been founded in 1922 by John Reith. Along with the NHS, the BBC remains one of the nation's greatest sources of pride.

In recent years there has been a move to modernise the service and new stations have been created to appeal to younger audiences, notably BBC3.

The BBC is largely funded from the TV licence, an annual charge that is required to watch TV programmes both on and off-line. A TV licence is not required to listen to BBC Radio programmes.

One of the best parts of BBC content is that no commercial advertising is used, meaning there are no ad breaks and you can enjoy programmes without interruption.

BBC TV programmes are available online through the *iPlayer* service and viewers must now login to use. In the near future, it is expected for which a TV licence is now required to watch both on and off-line.

One TV licence is required per home and the cost is currently £150.50/year. If you move into a house-share you will be able to split the charge between occupants.

Parenting

Parental Leave

Mothers, fathers and partners are eligible for parental leave and pay when they have a baby or adopt. Leave for mothers is known as *Maternity Leave* and can last up to one year. There are statutory (legal) minimums that an employer must pay but many employers will pay much more. The amount will depend on your length of service, organisation, current salary and whether you are employed or self-employed.

If your partner is having a baby, adopting or adopting through a surrogacy arrangement you may be eligible for

Paternity Pay and Leave. This is up to two weeks of paid leave. There is a statutory minimum amount but many employers will pay your normal wage.

Shared Leave and Pay

In 2015 the UK introduced *Shared Parental Leave and Pay*, a way of sharing leave between parents if having or adopting a child. Up to 50 weeks of leave can be shared, either in blocks or all in one go.

Most commonly this will mean that the mother will be able to give some of her parental leave to the father. For instance, the mother may be a higher earner than the father so rather than taking 7 months leave may take 6 months, go back to work and transfer 1 month to the father. Since shared parental leave was launched the take-up has been low, but use will likely increase as awareness increases and employers become more supportive.

Childcare

The cost of a nursery, pre-school or childminder will vary considerably between towns and cities. The most popular places will fill up quickly and it is advisable to reserve places in advance.

If you are struggling with the cost then think creatively. For instance, it may be cheaper for a parent to work fewer or compressed hours rather than pay for as much childcare.

Government support

The government provides financial support to help with the cost of looking after children. These payments are set depending on the number of children, parental income, working hours, other benefits and how much you spend on childcare.

- Child Benefit - Help based on the number of children.
- Tax free childcare - The government refunds the basic rate of tax back onto money used to pay directly for childcare, up to £2,000 per year.
- Free childcare - Children aged 3 and 4 get up to 30 hours of free childcare per week.

Employer benefits

Many employers have child-friendly benefits including flexible working, childcare vouchers and onsite nurseries. When considering a new job, it is advisable to check what is available.

Food shopping

Food shopping is dominated by supermarket chains and most people do their weekly shop at their local supermarket. Home delivery services are now available from most of the major UK supermarkets and can help to save time.

Utilities

The quote that 'in this world, nothing can be said to be certain, except death and taxes' is attributed to a letter written by the United States Founding Father Benjamin Franklin in 1789. Household bills can probably be added to that list of certainties. While utility bills, essential household bills, can't be avoided there are some smart ways to reduce their cost.

The largest household bills you are likely to face is for the supply of electricity, gas and water. Most properties will use gas for heating and hot water, and electricity for power. In many modern properties there may be no mains gas supply, everything will be electric. In rural areas, bottled gas is often used where there is no mains supply.

Generally, electricity is more expensive than gas as most of the electricity supply is generated by burning gas.

In England, Wales and Northern Ireland households pay for water and wastewater collection directly to the supplier. In Scotland a water charge is included with Council Tax You may be able to get a water meter that could allow you to pay less.

Types of bill

- Unmetered bills - The bill is estimated based on several factors including the size and location of the property. This is the default method for paying for domestic water and is used by most homes.
- Metered bills - The bill is calculated based on the actual usage of electricity, gas or water. It can also include a fixed charge. Metered connections can be

paid using a variety of methods including monthly, annually and prepayment meters.

In most cases, it will be cheaper to install a meter than to continue with an unmetered bill. This is because unmetered bills assume generous usage to ensure that supplier costs are covered. Installation of a meter can usually be requested to the supplier. In rented accommodation, tenants will need to seek their landlord's permission.

Simple ways to save

- Pay by monthly direct debit - There may be a discount paying monthly than paying quarterly or annually. Another advantage is that you can understand your usage and regular payments are easier to plan for. A large one-off bill may send you into your overdraft.

- Go paperless - Suppliers often provide a discount. Paperless doesn't mean you don't get bills but that your bills are digital and you need to login to view and download them. Occasionally paper bills are required as proof of address but these can be ordered.

- Be efficient - For electricity and gas consider using an efficient boiler, fit energy saving light bulbs (compact fluorescents or LEDs), switch off appliances when not in use, use heating controls for specific hours. For water get some water saving freebies from your water company; low flow shower heads, tap aerators to reduce tap flows, toilet cistern water reduction bags and shower timers. You can also reduce running taps by washing dishes using a bowl and brush your teeth without a constant flow.

- Sign up for a smart meter. Smart meters provide accurate digital billing and real-time information to the consumer. Smart meters are currently being rolled out across the UK, with the aim of every household using one by 2020. Tenants can contact their supplier to see if they are eligible.

Tip! *Tap water is safe to drink, so there is no need to buy bottled water. The high mineral content in the water of some regions (known as hard water) can be an acquired taste. A water filter can remove the minerals and improve the taste. Water filters can be fitted on the mains pipe entering the property or at the tap.*

Alternatively, bottles and jugs with in-built filters are available.

Council Tax

Council Tax is charged by the local authority (council) you live in and is used to fund local services such as schools, waste collection, roads and street lighting. For those moving from North America, it is equivalent to a property tax. Rates are based on historical house prices, that don't necessarily reflect the modern cost of living in an area.

Generally, a typical property will have an annual council tax bill of between £1,100 to £1,500. It's best to pay monthly by direct debit and to monitor your account online to ensure no mistakes are made.

Discounts are given in the following circumstances

- Students pay no council tax - A bill may still be sent to the property and an exemption can be applied for by providing proof of student status.
- Single occupants get 25% off - This will also apply if no one at the property is over 18, for diplomats and in some other situations.

***Tip!** Keep hold of paper bills as they are often required as proof of address for tenancy agreements.*

Internet

The internet is now considered an essential utility for households. Broadband internet delivered wirelessly is now the norm and there are ambitious plans to deliver superfast broadband across the nation. At present speeds can vary considerably between urban and rural areas.

New customers can often be enticed by lower prices for an initial period, usually the first six months or year. However, it is important to consider how prices will rise beyond this period.

To find the best internet deal search on one of the Price Comparison Sites such as *GoCompare*, *Compare the Market* or *Money Supermarket*.

Insurance

The issue of whether to take out insurance or not is one of those topics that divides opinion. Some think it is a worthwhile investment both financially and for peace of mind, while other think that it is money wasted.

The biggest recommendation I would make is to take out some type of contents insurance. As a minimum, this will typically cover accidental damage and thefts inside the home. If you own a valuable bike, laptop or jewellery it will be worthwhile. For home owners, it is advisable to take out full building's insurance. For those renting, buildings insurance will be taken out by your landlord.

Contents insurance can often be extended with additional cover. The most useful of these is the insurance of personal items outside the home. This could cost as little as a few more pounds per months and cover your mobile phone, laptop, bike or another item in the event of damage or theft. If you have this additional cover, it will probably mean you do not need to take out insurance for your new iPhone for instance, potentially saving you a considerable amount.

Libraries

It may come as a shock to the younger generation, but there is an established system for reading books without paying a penny; the humble local library. Libraries have modernised in recent years with more digital services and many hosting community events.

You can borrow library e-books and a limited range of audiobooks through your smartphone, tablet and computer using an app.

Saving for a rainy day

Putting money away into some type of a savings account may not be your top priority, but it is an important part of becoming financially sustainable.

For instance, moving from one place to another can be very expensive and savings can help to cushion the blow. Using savings to move is preferable to getting into the overdraft of your bank account, that may charge each day you are overdrawn.

Overdrafts come in two flavours, authorised and unauthorised. If you have to use your overdraft make sure you only use the authorised amount that will either be free or have a lower daily rate than an unauthorised overdraft.

It is also sensible to keep money aside for unexpected situations in an 'emergency fund'. A last-minute trip to visit an ill relative or a broken laptop are examples of unexpected situations that could require last minute access to cash. A useful rule of thumb is to have three months' worth of outgoings in an easy to access savings account.

The best way I have found to save money is to set up a monthly standing order from my current account into a separate savings account that I can't easily access. The standing order is set for the beginning of the month, just after I get paid at the end of the previous month. In fact, all my direct debits and standing orders are setup to run just after I get paid and this allows me to easily see what I have left for the upcoming month.

It's helpful to know the difference between standing orders and direct debits. A standing order is a regular payment you set up to a person or organisation, while a direct debit is a regular payment you authorise an organisation to take from your account. A key difference is that you have control over a standing order, so can easily amend or cancel it, while you don't have this control with a direct debit. Bills are usually paid by direct debit and a utility company that puts up their price, will let you know about the increase but you don't need to change the amount as they will manage this

Different types of savings accounts

- Easy access savings accounts - Easy to setup and withdraw money from. Useful for savings for short term goals.
- Regular savings accounts - Decide on a regular amount to transfer into the savings account. Holders typically can't pay in more than the agreed amount but this setup is useful for those who struggle to save consistently. Best for medium term saving.
- Individual Savings Accounts (ISAs) - Tax-free savings accounts offered by all banks. ISAs come in different forms including Cash ISAs, Stocks & Shares ISAs, Innovative Finance ISAs and Lifetime ISAs (LISAs). There is an annual limit of what can be saved, with the limit including any money paid in and subsequently removed before interest is paid. LISAs are designed to save for the deposit of your first home or retirement, paying interest plus a 25% bonus each year.

- Bonds - Longer term saving option that offers a higher interest rate. The longer you will be happy to lock your cash away for the higher the interest rate.

10. Going out and staying in

'What passes for cookery in England is an abomination. It is putting cabbages in water. It is roasting meat till it is like leather. It is cutting off delicious skins of vegetables. A whole French family could live on what an English cook throws away.'

Virginia Woolf (1882-1941), author

Getting a good deal

Haggling over prices is generally uncommon but will still happen in street markets. However, even in a shop, there is nothing to lose by asking for a better deal as the worst someone can say is no. Often this approach even works in well-known stores, as a store will often rather sell you something than let you walk out buying nothing.

It's almost always worth looking around for the best price for the level of quality you want. Except for a few items such as stamps, the price of an item will vary by shop. Some stores have price matching guarantees, whereby they will match a price offered by a rival if it is available at a lower price.

In recent years, the world of e-commerce has taken off and there are now a multitude of online services offering discounts. It's worth having a dose of healthy scepticism when prices are dropped as they may have been inflated to begin with.

Here are some to look out for

- *Groupon* - Sign-up to the email newsletter for regular discounts or use discount codes online.
- *Money Saving Expert* - Sign up for the email newsletter and browse the online resources.

Cultural events

The UK has a diverse cultural scene with events and activities taking place throughout the year. Helpfully many of these events are free or low-cost to attend.

Here are some favourites for locals and tourists alike.

- Chinese New Year - Marked by a Chinese New Year Parade, performances and of course food. There are sizeable Chinatowns in London, Liverpool, Manchester and Birmingham. Buffets are particularly popular.

- New Year's Day Parade - Celebrate the 1st day of the year watching dancers, acrobats, cheerleaders, marching bands and historic vehicles passing through the streets.
- Open Days - Free entry to buildings that are normally closed to the public or charge. Advance booking required for some venues.
- Pride Parade - Celebration of the UK's LGBT+ community.
- St Patrick's Day - Many lively free events celebrate Ireland's patron saint.

One of the best aspects of the UK's cultural scene is that national museums and art galleries are centrally funded so that they are free for general admission. Special exhibitions may change and donations of £5-10 are encouraged. Many of the national museums are in the capital cities but there are also situated elsewhere.

- British Museum - London
- Kelvingrove Art Gallery and Museum - Glasgow
- Museum of Childhood - London
- Museum of London - London
- National Gallery - London

- National Maritime Museum - London
- National Portrait Gallery - London
- Natural History Museum - London
- National Museums of Northern Ireland - across Northern Ireland
- National Museums of Scotland - across Scotland
- National Museum of Wales - Cardiff
- National Railway Museum - York
- National Science & Media Museum - Bradford
- Science Museum - London
- Tate - Dundee, Liverpool, London, St Ives
- Wellcome Collection - London
- Victoria & Albert - London

Other great websites to find ways to pass the time and to meet people

- Eventbrite - Discover a wide range of events and groups
- Meet-up - Groups cover a wide range of Interests

Tip! *Sign up to the email newsletter for venues you are interested in, for updates on deals and special events.*

The movies

Going to the cinema is one of the nation's favourite pastimes but it can get pricey to see the latest release in the city centre at a big multiplex cinema.

If you plan to go to the cinema on a regular basis you may want to get a cinema membership through a chain such as *PictureHouse* or *Cineworld*. It's worth working out how many films you would need to see in order to get your money's worth.

Matinee (afternoon) and weekday tickets are typically cheaper than evening and weekend tickets and students can get large discounts.

Tip! *If you regularly see films in 3D, then remember to take glasses so you don't need to buy new ones each time you go.*

Dining out

Eating out is one of the most enjoyable ways to spend an evening and the nation is doing more and more of it.

Prices can vary hugely between local restaurants in the suburbs and Michelin star offerings in the centre. As well as an increase in eating out, there has been a huge rise in the number of people ordering home deliveries using mobile apps such as *Deliveroo*, *Just Eat and Uber Eats*.

Eating out and meeting friends over a pint can be one of the great joys in life. Try out where the locals drink as it is bound to be more affordable than the new hipster bar around the corner.

The pub

The pub (another word for a bar) is a British institution. The UK is famous for gin production and pubs are a great place to socialise over a drink. It's common to go for a drink after work to celebrate birthdays, project success or simply the end of the working week.

A spirit e.g. gin & mixer will typically cost £4-7, a pint of beer £3-6 and a glass of house wine £3-6.

The cheapest drinks will always be found where the locals drink. Alternatively, if you want a night in, off-licences and supermarkets will sell alcohol for a fraction of the price.

Here are some cost pub chains with low prices that can be found across the country.

- Nicholson's pubs
- Sam Smith's pubs
- Wetherspoons pubs
- Young's pubs

Keeping active

Taking part in some type of regular exercise will boost your physical and mental health.

Gym memberships can often cost a lot but you can often get special deals or no joining fee offers. Memberships prices will vary by location and by gym company with many now offering 24-hour access.

Urban areas have a surprising number of green spaces and water features. Visiting a park is a free way to change your surroundings, boost your physical and mental health. Many parks have cafés, activities and events to keep you busy.

If you enjoy running or want to get into running then try out your local *Park Run*. *Park Runs* are free, weekly 5K runs that can be found in parks in most towns and cities.

Your time is recorded and you can track your performance online. An alternative is *GoodGym*, which combines work-outs with doing good deeds in the local community such as assisting the elderly or environmental clean-ups.

Tip! *Gyms typically charge no joining fees for joining in January. This is perfect for those who put on a few pounds over the festive break.*

Theatreland

Britain has a world class theatre scene, but you don't need to break the bank to be able to see a show.

Tips to find cheap theatre tickets

- Choose a less popular time such as a weekday matinee performance.
- Know thy seats - Seats further from the stage on the ground (the stalls) will cost less than seats closer. Seats at the back of one of the upper levels will be the cheapest. Seats with a restricted view may be even cheaper.

- If you have a large group, speak to the box office or check online if you are eligible for a group discount. The definition of a group will be set by the theatre. Several shows have specific group deals.

- Buy directly from the theatre box office - Avoid pesky booking fees.

- Search for last minute tickets - *TKTS* (online/Leicester Square), *TodayTIX, Last Minute.*

- Enter a lottery. Some popular productions such as *The Lion King, Hamilton, Book of Mormon, Harry Potter and the Cursed Child* and *Aladdin* have regular lotteries for discounted tickets. The lotteries may be entered through the website, at the box office or using an app.

Finding the one

The dating world has moved online and there is now a range of paid and free sites to help you meet that special one. Some sites offer a mix of free and paid services.

Popular online dating sites/apps

- Bumble
- Ok Cupid
- eHarmony

- Lovestruck
- Match
- Tinder

11. Settle in the UK

'The important thing about having lots of things to remember is that you've got to go somewhere afterwards where you can remember them, you see? You've got to stop. You haven't really been anywhere until you've got back home.'

Terry Pratchett (1948-2015), author

Deciding to stay

Been in the UK on a visa and want to apply to stay? Great, the UK would like to welcome you. Immigrants make a huge contribution to the economy, culture and vibrancy of the UK.

You may have been thinking about settling in the UK ever since you arrived or perhaps it is a recent feeling. Things are falling into place and you feel like you are at home now. For some, settling may be more of a practical decision. You have a good job, you have friends and maybe some family here, so you would like to continue along the same trajectory.

It's important to consider that there are upsides and downsides to staying long term in any country. It is recommended you don't decide to settle in the UK on a whim and instead give it some serious consideration.

Life in the UK test

If you want to apply for settlement or Citizenship then you will be asked to sit the *Life in the UK test*. The test consists of 24 questions about British traditions and customs.

You can register to take the test on the government gateway website. There are many books and online resources to help you prepare for the test.

Applying for settlement

The right to live and work in the UK permanently is known as settlement. Settlement is also known as Indefinite Leave to Remain (ILR). The conditions for an individual to transition from their visa to settlement will vary.

Once you have gained settlement you no longer need to apply new visas or the Health Surcharge. However, you will still not have a British passport so will have to use your existing passport to travel.

Becoming a British Citizen

Once you have gained settlement in the UK, you may wish to apply for British Citizenship. Becoming a British Citizen is also known as naturalisation.

The benefits of gaining Citizenship over settlement include the right to a British passport and more voting rights.

The UK does allow dual nationality. This means you can be a British Citizen and a citizen of another country. However, you may find you have to renounce your previous nationality if your country doesn't recognise dual nationality.

Once you are accepted to become a British Citizen you will be invited to attend a Citizenship Ceremony. Ceremonies are arranged by your local authority and groups of new citizens attend together.

While the ceremony is a formal requirement, you could also see it as a celebration that you have made it this far. After spending many hours completing paperwork over several years and spending thousands of pounds, I think you may as well have a bit of a party, safe in the knowledge that you won't need to go through that again. Well done!

Help make this book better

If you have enjoyed this book please consider writing a review. Reviews can really help other decide what to start reading. Positive reviews are of course preferred but I will take anything I can get.

I have written this book under my own steam (what a British phrase) and may have missed out something important to you. If so, can you please let me know by emailing me at movingbooksnews@gmail.com. What would make the difference to you? All feedback will be appreciated.

Finally, if you enjoyed this book you may also like my other book *Moving to London: Essential Advice for Moving and Living on a Budget.*

Website:

https://movingtolondon.blog

Resources

The organisations mentioned above and a few others are listed below. They are generally listed in the order mentioned in the text.

Routes into the UK

UK Visas & Immigration

https://www.gov.uk/government/organisations/uk-visas-and-immigration

EU Citizens

https://www.gov.uk/guidance/status-of-eu-nationals-in-the-uk-what-you-need-to-know

Commonwealth Citizens

https://www.gov.uk/right-of-abode

First steps

Government information & services

https://www.gov.uk

Apply for a National Insurance number

https://www.gov.uk/apply-national-insurance-number

Check your National Insurance record

https://www.gov.uk/check-national-insurance-record

Find a health service e.g. doctor, dentist

http://www.nhs.uk/service-search

NHS Choices

http://www.nhs.uk/pages/home.aspx

City Sightseeing Bus Tours

https://city-sightseeing.com/en/home

SANDEMANs Free Walking Tours

http://www.neweuropetours.eu

British Council English resources

http://learnenglish.britishcouncil.org/en

Finding a place to call home

FIDI

https://www.fidi.org

Europcar

https://www.europcar.co.uk

Enterprise

https://www.enterprise.co.uk

Hertz

https://www.hertz.co.uk

Zip Car

https://www.zipcar.co.uk

Enterprise Car Club

https://www.enterprisecarclub.co.uk

Packing Boxes

http://www.packingboxes.co.uk

The Man Van

http://www.themanvan.co.uk

Tenancy Deposit Protection scheme

https://www.gov.uk/tenancy-deposit-protection/overview

Airbnb

https://www.airbnb.co.uk

SpareRoom

https://www.spareroom.co.uk

EasyRoommate

https://uk.easyroommate.com

Movebubble

https://www.movebubble.com

Openrent

https://www.openrent.co.uk

Roomi

https://roomiapp.com

Gum Tree

https://www.gumtree.com/property-to-rent

London Landlord Accreditation Scheme

http://www.londonlandlords.org.uk

National Landlord Association

https://landlords.org.uk/tenants

Rightmove

http://www.rightmove.co.uk

Zoopla

https://www.zoopla.co.uk

Freecycle groups

https://www.freecycle.org/browse/UK

Affordable housing options

https://www.helptobuy.gov.uk

Working in the UK

Adecco

http://www.adecco.co.uk

Blue Arrow

https://www.bluearrow.co.uk

Hays

https://www.hays.co.uk

Michael Page

https://www.michaelpage.co.uk

Indeed

https://www.indeed.co.uk

Jobsite

www.jobsite.co.uk

Monster

https://www.monster.co.uk

Reed

https://www.reed.co.uk/jobs

Universal Jobmatch

https://jobsearch.direct.gov.uk

Money Advice Service guide

https://www.moneyadviceservice.org.uk/en/articles/understand
ing-your-payslip

UK Tax Codes

https://www.gov.uk/tax-codes/overview

Tax relief for employees

https://www.gov.uk/tax-relief-for-employees

Check your record

https://www.gov.uk/check-national-insurance-record

State Pension

https://www.gov.uk/new-state-pension

Workplace pensions

https://www.gov.uk/workplace-pensions/about-workplace-pensions

Education, Education, Education

Nursery places

https://www.gov.uk/find-nursery-school-place

School admissions

https://www.gov.uk/schools-admissions

England inspections reports

https://www.gov.uk/government/organisations/ofsted

Wales inspection reports

https://www.estyn.gov.wales

Scotland inspection reports

https://education.gov.scot

N. Ireland inspection reports

https://www.etini.gov.uk

England performance tables

https://www.gov.uk/school-performance-tables

Wales performance tables

http://mylocalschool.wales.gov.uk

Scotland performance tables

http://www.gov.scot/Topics/Statistics/Browse/School-Education

N. Ireland performance tables

https://www.education-ni.gov.uk/services/schools-plus

Getting around

Citymapper app

https://citymapper.com

Tube map app

https://www.mapway.com/apps/tube-map-london-underground

Google Maps

https://www.google.co.uk/maps

Oyster Cards

https://oyster.tfl.gov.uk/oyster/entry.do

Commuter Club

https://www.commuterclub.co.uk

Rail cards

https://www.railcard.co.uk

My taxi app

https://uk.mytaxi.com

Gett app

https://gett.com/uk

Uber app

https://www.uber.com/en-GB/ride

Everyday practicalities

TV licence

http://www.tvlicensing.co.uk

Council Tax

https://www.gov.uk/council-tax/working-out-your-council-tax

Shared Parental Leave and Pay

https://www.gov.uk/shared-parental-leave-and-pay

Child Tax Credits

https://www.gov.uk/child-tax-credit

Consumer protection rights

https://www.gov.uk/consumer-protection-rights

Going out and staying in

Groupon

https://www.groupon.co.uk

Money Saving Expert

https://www.moneysavingexpert.com

Open House London

http://openhouselondon.org.uk

Park Run

http://www.parkrun.org.uk

TKTS

http://www.tkts.co.uk/about-tkt

Today Tix

https://www.todaytix.com

Last Minute

http://www.lastminute.com

Settle in the UK

Life in the UK Test

https://www.gov.uk/life-in-the-uk-test

Apply to settle in the UK

https://www.gov.uk/settle-in-the-uk

Apply for British Citizenship

https://www.gov.uk/browse/citizenship

Made in the USA
Monee, IL
24 April 2022

95323444R00080